More Than Enough
With Plenty Left Over

More Than Enough
With Plenty Left Over

Jack Holt

Printed in the United States of America

Publishing services by Selah Publishing Group, LLC, Indiana. The views expressed or implied in this work do not necessarily reflect those of Selah Publishing Group.

ISBN: 1-58930-156-0
Library of Congress Control Number: 2005904355

Dedicated to Joyce

I want to dedicate this book to my beloved wife Joyce, who's been a support to me over all these years in the things of God. She has never sought after recognition for herself, but has always been behind the scenes helping in the work of the ministry. I never could have accomplished all that I've accomplished in the Lord without her support. She is God's gift to me. Joyce has helped balance out my life and is my closest friend. The Bible says to give honor to whom honor is due, and she has earned great honor not only in my sight, but also within our church. She is the First Lady of River of Life Fellowship and I am blessed having more than enough with plenty left over with Joyce by my side.

Your loving husband Jack

Contents

Introduction

As a man thinks, so he is.
PROVERBS 23:7

In my dealings with people over the years, I have found that many people have mixed-up thinking set in their minds. As a result, their lives are skewed off course and filled with wrong perceptions about themselves and God—especially where money is concerned.

The truth is God wants every believer to have more than enough with plenty left over—and with Him right in the middle of it all.

Through the pages of this book, I hope to help you open or unlock your mind to the truth of God's Word by showing you the steps that will teach you to have faith without limits, to have boldness to ask God for what you need and desire, and to always remember where the answers and provisions come from in life.

But it all starts with your thinking.

Consider the possibilities of your life if only your thinking was bigger, and how God could use you if you had unlimited thinking. Whenever there is big vision there is big provision.

Introduction

If you will increase your vision, hopes and dreams for your family, your business, or your ministry, God will provide the provision for you. Keep reading and I'll show you how.

—Jack Holt
River of Life Fellowship, Kent, Washington

CHAPTER 1

God Really Wants You to Have *More Than Enough With Plenty Leftover*

Imagine a church whose members are so prosperous—they have more than enough with plenty left over—that people in need come to them and not the government for help!

Imagine a church whose members are so full of wisdom, so strong in Christ-like character that when people enter their Sunday services, the manifestation of God's glory is so intense, visitors are overwhelmed. They recognize an atmosphere they've never known before.

Imagine a church whose married couples are so happy and fulfilled, so faithful and committed that everyone wants to know their secret.

Imagine a church whose families are so strong, whose children and teens are so mentally and emotionally stable and well-rounded, that everyone wants to know how they are doing it all so right!

Sound like a dream?

It is.

It is God's dream.

And God never dreams anything that isn't possible.

God Wants to Give You What You *Want*— Not Just What You *Need*

I know that you and I can live in God's dream. We can live prosperously in every area of our lives.

No, it won't happen overnight...but if you'll embark on the journey of walking with God in how you manage the money He entrusts to you, change for the better will occur step by step in your life.

I know that you and I can live in God's dream. We can live prosperously in every area of our lives.

I know what I'm talking about. What my wife, Joyce and I have today is a far cry from where we first started.

When we first stepped out in ministry, we were so poor we joked that we spelled it with three o's! P-o-o-o-r! We were so broke, a neighbor—who was moved with compassion and fortunately worked at a grocery store—brought us all the expired hot dogs and meats the store threw away. That's how we ate every week.

God Really Wants You to Have
More Than Enough With Plently Left Over

It was a hard season in our lives, but we kept living by God's Word, obeying His precepts and trusting in His faithfulness. As we did, little by little, year after year, our lives improved. Today, we are so blessed. We are so grateful for all God has given us— and it is what convinces us that God can do anything for anyone. All you have to do is serve Him with your whole heart and live by what He tells you to do.

> *God loves His children and He wants to lavishly give to them.*

So many times, well-meaning Christians don't understand God's intentions to bless them, mostly because they don't really understand what God's word actually says. For example, I've heard believers say, "God may not give you want you want, but He will always give you what you need."

Where is that in the Bible?

It isn't.

And as a result of believing wrong information, many Christians live their lives convinced God is only obligated to provide the basic necessities of life. They believe that having the basics met is evidence of walking in the perfect will of God.

Nothing could be further from the truth.

God loves His children and He wants to lavishly give to them.

Psalm 34:10 says, "The young lions *lack* and suffer hunger; But those who seek the LORD shall not *lack* any good thing" (*New King James Version*).[1]

In the phrase, "the young lions lack," the original Hebrew meaning of *lack* refers to being destitute in the animal kingdom. Like most animal young, lion

13

cubs are not able to feed themselves and are depen-
dent upon the parents to provide for them. If there is
a famine or drought, the young lions will suffer and
be without the basics necessary for survival. Consequently, they will perish.

The second time *lack* is used in Psalm 34:10, it
has a completely different Hebrew root. Its meaning
conveys the understanding that you shall not lack the
things you want in life...or the good things you want
out of life.

Do you see the difference?

When we understand what the Bible really says
about matters, it opens up to us understanding of
the goodness of God. His intentions for our lives are
always good.

Psalm 84:11 states, "For the Lord God is a sun
and shield; The Lord will give grace and glory; No
good thing will He withhold from those who walk
uprightly" (*New King James Version*).[2]

Do you hear the heart beat of God in this verse?
Do you hear His goodness?

There is nothing—that is a good thing—too good
for you to have. There is no size of house, no make or
model of car, no great marriage, no healthy relationship, no healthy body...that is too good for you to have!

---

*There is nothing which is good
that is too good for you!*

I'll say it one more time! There is nothing which
is good that is too good for you! No size of salary...no
material possession...is too good for you as long as
you are doing what God has called you to do.

God Really Wants You to Have
More Than Enough With Plently Left Over

For years I've heard people misinterpret scriptures like Psalm 84:11. A lack of understanding has robbed them of what God truly intends for every Christian.

One of the most popular passages in the Bible is another widely misunderstood message. Psalm 23:1 begins, "The Lord is my shepherd; I shall not want."[3] Believers have developed the wrong idea that if a person is spiritual then they will not want anything.

Again, if you don't understand the original Hebrew meaning, you will be left believing the wrong information.

The original meaning of this passage is: "The Lord is my Shepherd; I shall not be in lack." Because God is my shepherd, I will not lack anything.

Jesus understood the original Hebrew. He was raised knowing how to read it. That's why He could promise us "If you abide in Me, and My words abide in you, you will ask what you desire, and it shall be done for you" (John 15:7, *New King James Version*).[4]

The original Greek—which is the language in which the New Testament was first written—writes this verse as a *command* to ask what you wish or want. Imagine! He has commanded us to ask for what we wish or want!

God has commanded us to ask for what we wish or want!

If you are remaining in His love, and His Word is remaining in you, the Lord finds great pleasure in your prayer life bearing much fruit. He loves to grant what you ask!

Our God is wonderful, and He desires to do more than just meet your basic needs. He wants to provide for your wants, as long as they are good.

Walk with me through the journey of this book and I will show you more of God's marvelous ways. I'll teach you how to think like God thinks when it comes to your money and His plan for your life. I will teach you how to have more than enough with plenty left over.

CHAPTER 2

God's Dream For Your Life

God has a dream for His Church and God has a dream for your individual life. It's a plan to prosper you in every area of your life. He wants your marriage great, your kids happy and healthy, your job pleasurable and everything increasing continually.

Jeremiah 29:11 is His Word to you: "'For I know the plans I have for you,' declares the LORD, 'plans to prosper you and not to harm you, plans to give you hope and a future'" (*New International Version*).[5]

But there are things you and I must do in order to receive the abundance God wants us to have.

First and foremost, we must position ourselves to receive. In Matthew 6:33, Jesus tells us exactly how to do that: "But seek ye first the kingdom of God, and his righteousness; and all these things shall be added unto you." (*New King James Version*)[6]

When we seek God above all else in our lives, He blesses us. He gives us the desires of our hearts. In Psalm 37:4, David wrote: "Delight yourself in the Lord and he will give you the desires of your heart" (*New International Version*).[7]

He protects our assets: "And I will rebuke the devourer for your sakes, so that he will not destroy the fruit of your ground; nor shall the vine fail to bear fruit for you in the field, says the LORD of hosts" (Malachi 3:11 *New King James Version*).[8]

When we seek God above all else in our lives, He blesses us.

He protects our families from tragedy and harm: "If you make the Most High your dwelling even the Lord, who is my refuge then no harm will befall you, no disaster will come near your tent [your home]. For he will command his angels concerning you to guard you in all your ways; they will lift you up in their hands, so that you will not strike your foot against a stone" (Psalm 91:9-12, *New International Version*).[9]

The Power of Putting Him First

Part of seeking God first, of putting Him and His interests before our own, is giving to Him the first fruits of all our labor. Since most of modern culture doesn't farm, we can't literally give the first of our harvest, so we give God the tithe off our income. The tithe, by Bible definition, is 10 percent. It's the first fruits of our labor.

It's easy and natural to think: *I don't want to hear this. I'm having financial troubles as it is.*

But I have to say it.

And you need to hear it.

God is not trying to take your money...or anything else from you. He is trying to get something to you. He's trying to prosper you—and when you tithe, it opens up the windows of Heaven over every area of your life.

I feel so strongly about this because the root to a lot of the problems in marriages and relationships is money related. Through my years of being in ministry and counseling Christians, I have found that 90 percent of people's problems have to do with money— and usually the love of money.

I feel so strongly about this because the root to a lot of the problems in marriages and relationships is money related.

Oftentimes, amongst couples I've counseled, the conversation goes something like this:

Wife: "Well, he never gives me time. He's always working."

Husband: "It takes so much nowadays to make it, and I want the good life."

Nine times out of ten, couples who talk like this are not tithing. Because they aren't tithing off their increase, they can't keep up with the hole in their pocket. So the husband—or both of them—has to work around the clock to make ends meet.

Other couples I've counseled simply never have enough money. They are always broke. I understand we all have times when we're not on the mountaintops of life, but it is one thing to go through the valley, and it's another to make your home in the valley. People who make their home in the valley aren't putting God first. God wants you to go through the valley, to the place of financial increase.

God wants every believer to have money. He says in His Word that the love of money is the root of all evil, not the money itself (1 Timothy 6:10). Money is good. It's helpful. It's necessary. And if you tithe, God is obligated to bless you!

It's when people become materialistic-minded that they get out of God's will. First Timothy 6:9-10 warns us: "People who want to get rich fall into temptation and a trap and into many foolish and harmful desires that plunge men into ruin and destruction. For the love of money is a root of all kinds of evil. Some people, eager for money, have wandered from the faith and pierced themselves with many griefs" (*New International Version*).[10]

---

*M*oney isn't the main thing in life. It's the tool to do the main thing.

The word *desires* in this verse is from a root word meaning "a very corrupt desire." It is describing the kind of desire that comes from reasoning, consumes your life, drives you to acquire wealth, and thrives as your first priority in life.

That is the love of money the Bible describes as the root of all evil.

Godly gain—money honestly acquired by someone who seeks first the kingdom of God— is a blessing. Proverbs 10:22 says "The blessing of the Lord makes one rich, and He adds no sorrow with it. (*New King James Version*)[11]

Money isn't the main thing in life.

It's the tool to do the main thing.

Why God Wants You Prospering

God wants you blessed with plenty left over because He loves you and His heart and thoughts are always toward you.

But He has another reason as well.

God wants you prosperous—first and foremost—so you can support the work of the ministry. He wants you to be ready at any time to give to every good work (2 Corinthians 9:8).[12] He wants you to help further His kingdom in the earth—which means to win souls and help believers grow into maturity. Obviously this is accomplished in a multitude of ways. There are ministries all over the world—and in your community—who feed the poor, preach the gospel, pray for the sick, and minister in so many practical ways, all the while demonstrating the saving power of Jesus Christ. And they can only do what they do when God's people give to every good work as the Holy Spirit leads them—out of the excess resources they have accumulated.

Put Your Money Where It Can Grow

Whatever you have in the bank today can grow, if you put God first in your life and demonstrate that by tithing to Him...and then beyond the tithe, as His Holy Spirit leads, give to good works.

When you honor God with your first fruits, He honors you by increasing you...financially, socially, relationally...in every area of your life.

That's His commitment to you.

But regardless of what your bank balance is right now, always remain content. Contentment is a force that will take you far. First Timothy 6:6-7 says, "But godliness with contentment is great gain. For we brought nothing into the world, and we can take nothing out of it" *(New International Version).*[13]

Whatever size house you have today, be content. Whatever kind of car you have today, be content.

Contentment is power. It is "God sufficiency." By that I mean God gave you all things that pertain to life and godliness when He saved you, and it's all on the inside of you right now. Second Peter 1:3 says: "Seeing that His divine power has granted to us everything pertaining to life and godliness, through the true knowledge of Him who called us by His own glory and excellence" *(New American Standard).*[14]

So, if you need money to pay a bill, you have on the inside of you what it takes to have more than enough with plenty left over. Trust Him, believe Him, seek Him and do what He says—and the money will come.

Build up your power, wisdom and inner strength by being content now, regardless of what you have or don't have. First Timothy 6:8 goes on to say, "But if we have food and clothing, we will be content with that."[15]

Yes, God wants you prosperous. Yes, He wants you to have more than enough with plenty left over. But He also wants you to be content with what you already have.

Attitude is just as critical to God as outward obedience.

For example, if you tithe, but with the wrong attitude, you are only partially obeying. Second Corinthians 9:7 says it clearly: "Each man should give what he has decided in his heart to give, not reluctantly or under compulsion, for God loves a cheerful giver" (*New International Version*).[16]

---

*A*ttitude is just as critical to God as outward obedience.

Use Your Tool

God wants you to always be content with what you have, while continuing to increase at the same time. He wants you to always put Him first and to give into every good work He tells you to. He wants you seeing money as a tool and using it as a tool.

God wants you to have money, but money to never have you—all because He wants you positioned to have more than enough with plenty left over so you can give to the work of the ministry. That is His number one reason for wanting you prosperous.

---

*G*od wants you to have money, but money to never have you

I liken it to dental floss. No one tries to store up dental floss. We use it once and throw it away.
Money is like the floss. It's meant to be used...not hoarded. It's something to make the journey of life better. So use it like that. Use it to make the ride

through life more enjoyable, because like everything material in our lives, at the end of the age, it will be burned up with fire.

---

*M*oney is like the floss. It's meant to be used...not hoarded.

God wants you to have the resources at hand at any given moment, to do the work of the ministry, to give opportunity to people, to be a blessing to people. As you do with what you have now and what is to come in the future, He'll always make sure all of your needs are met.

This and so much more is what I will show you through the pages of this book. God wants you to never again expect to be broke, but to anticipate how He will increase you. His name in the Hebrew language is *El Shaddai*, which translates as "the God who is more than enough"—and I believe He is also the one who wants you to have more than enough with plenty left over.

First Timothy 6:17-19 says it all well: "Command those who are rich in this present age not to be haughty, nor to trust in uncertain riches but in the living God, who gives us richly all things to enjoy. Let them do good, that they be rich in good works, ready to give, willing to share, storing up for themselves a good foundation for the time to come, that they may lay hold on eternal life" (*New King James Version*).[17]

Having more than enough with plenty left over is God's dream for you. His ways and instructions are always to get something to you...plenty for yourself and plenty to share.

CHAPTER 3

Accruing More Than Enough– It's a Process

I remember when I was young…dating and looking for just the right girl to marry. It was quite a process. First I had to find one even willing to go out with me! Then I had to dress and act like I never had before. I had to figure out what would impress a girl, and avoid everything that wouldn't. I had to learn to watch chick flicks—and act like I enjoyed them!

The bottom line was if I were to find a bride— you'll be glad to know I finally did and she's still the apple of my eye—I had to go through the process.

In the course of going through the process, I found my wife, Joyce. In our courtship, there was a turning point when she began to see me as the best thing that ever happened to her.

But that led to a new process.

I had to get up my nerve to ask her to marry me. Of course that wasn't the hardest part. The hardest part was once she said, "Yes!" I had to figure out how to afford her!

Seriously, my point is that finding the right woman or man to marry—for all of us—is a process. It doesn't happen overnight—and neither does the accrual of wealth.

When Joyce and I married, we didn't rent a limo. We had my old car. We didn't go to Hawaii for a weeklong honeymoon—we stayed one night in Seattle and the other night at Ocean Shores near our hometown of Seattle, where we were attacked by fleas. But we didn't care. We were in love. Then we came back Sunday night and went to work on Monday.

We loved God and served Him, but we weren't rich at all. As I said earlier, we were far from it. But we were consistent.

The reason most people don't accrue much is because they check out of the process way too soon. They don't remain consistent.

Finish the Process

Accruing wealth is a process that takes time. The reason most people don't accrue much is because they check out of the process way too soon. They don't remain consistent. They don't finish the process.

They get a little understanding, find out God wants them prosperous, but get mad or disappointed when it doesn't happen overnight.

Don't ever quit. You have to stay with the process of managing your money correctly. You have to stay with the process of stewardship, of worshipping God with your money—tithing according to the word, giving as the Holy Spirit leads you, doing your job as unto the Lord, and deciding responsibly how to spend and save.

If you will be faithful with the process, you will finish the process—and the blessings of God will fill your life.

I liken it to making a latte. I have a great little espresso machine and I enjoy making lattes for Joyce and me.

To make a good latte, I start with putting water in the machine. If I don't put water in the machine, I can't steam the milk, and I can't run the Espresso—so there's nothing to mix if I don't first start with water.

In other words, it's a process.

I have to put the water in first before I can begin the process of steaming the milk, and so on.

The water required for a good latte is like the Word of God. You have to put the Word of God into your marriage before you'll get any steam out of the relationship! You have to put the Word of God into your job before you receive your paycheck.

What do I mean by this?

Doing what God tells you to do in life, putting Him first in your life, doing your job with excellence. Colossians 3:23 tells us, "And whatever you do, do it heartily, as to the Lord and not to men" (*New King James Version*).[18] The results are God working through your wages, your company, through bonuses to increase you because you put Him first.

In your marriage, it is putting God's will first which includes forgiving every offense no matter how many times your husband or wife messes up. It's being faithful. It's being loving and honorable.

When you act according to God's principles, your job and your marriage—and all of your life—when you stay with the process, you reap the results...a blessed and prosperous life.

The Promise of Putting the Word First

John 15:7 says, "If you abide in Me, and My words abide in you, you will ask what you desire, and it shall be done for you" *(New King James Version).*[19]

Abide means "to remain, to take up residence." So God is saying in this verse that His Word is to remain in us. It's to be a consistent part of our lives. Our Christian faith is to be lived daily—not just at Christmas and Easter or in a time of crisis.

If we remain in His Word, then we can ask anything according to His will and it will be done for us.

Why? Because God is at work putting His will in our hearts as we remain in His Word. As we remain in His Word, His desires become our desires. Then, when we ask, we're asking according to the work He's doing in us...we're asking according to His will, and He grants our request.

The Apostle Paul wrote to the Philippians: "For it is God who is at work in you, both to will and to work for His good pleasure" (Philippians 2:13, *New American Standard).*[20]

God puts the initial desires—His good desires—in our hearts, then when we ask in faith as we abide in Him, He does what we ask.

That's powerful!

You literally have the power—and responsibility—to bring God's will to pass in the earth, all by remaining in His Word daily.

God puts the initial desires—His good desires—in our hearts, then when we ask in faith as we abide in Him, He does what we ask.

God is commanding us to live this way. It's not an option.

I know in my own life there are things burning in my spirit that I have to believe God for, things that I have to ask in faith for, because it would be a sin against God not to. God has put those desires in my heart, because He wants me to ask and believe Him to do them. They are His will in this earth.

What a responsibility and a privilege to cooperate with God Himself to accomplish His will in the earth! That's what He wants to do in you and through you too!

Filter Your Desires With God's Word

So how do you know which desires in your heart are God's and which are your will at work?

Use the Word to filter your desires.

For example, before a pilot takes off, he always goes through a checklist. In the same way, before you ask for what you want in life, go through the following checklist taken from the Word of God:

First, make sure you are walking in love with others. First John 3:22 says, "And whatever we ask we receive from Him, because we keep His commandments and do the things that are pleasing in His sight" (*New American Standard*).[21]

$\mathcal{U}$*se the Word to filter your desires.*

Is there anyone you have offense against? Is there anyone you hate or dislike and have talked about?

If there is, go make it right before you ask for the desires of your heart.

Second, don't ask for anything that isn't promised in the Bible. Romans 10:17 says, "So faith comes from hearing, and hearing by the word of Christ" (*New American Standard*).[22]

You can't have faith for something God hasn't provided faith for. In other words, you are in error if you say, "Well, I really desire that other man's wife."

Wrong. Faith for another man's wife isn't promised in the Bible. In fact, one of The Ten Commandments instructs you not to covet another man's wife. Another commandment tells us not to commit adultery. Desiring another man's wife is asking outside the guidelines of God's Word.

Simply put, if what you want isn't offered by God in His word, you have no business asking for it.

Third, check your attitude. Isaiah 1:19 says, "If you are willing and obedient, you shall eat the good of the land" (*New King James Version*).[23]

So if you are negative while you obey, then you won't eat the best God has for you. You won't get what you want. Wrong attitudes can block your getting the desires of your heart.

Fourth, make sure you are doing what God has told you to do. Psalm 127:1 says, "Unless the Lord builds the house, its builders labor in vain" (*New International Version*).[24]

What are you doing? Is it something God led you to do? Or, something you decided to do?

When you go through this checklist before you ask God for anything, and you take the steps necessary to ensure you're asking for the desires He's placed in your heart, you can ask and not doubt knowing He will give your request to you.

Asking for God's will for your life in faith is part of going through the process. It is part of not asking amiss and making it to your destiny in life—which is filled with more than enough with plenty left over.

James wrote: "Ye ask, and receive not, because ye ask amiss, that ye may consume it upon your lusts" (James 4:3 *King James Version*).[25]

Motive is everything to God.

Attitude is everything to God.

Genuine obedience is everything to God.

Finishing the process is everything to God.

Increase Your Favor With God

Part of the process of accruing wealth is increasing your favor with God. By this I mean you are to live in a way that is pleasing to God. You are to treat other people in ways that are pleasing to God. When you do, you increase in favor with Him. Jesus demonstrated this for us when He walked the earth.

When Jesus was only 12 years old, He went to the temple in Jerusalem and began to ask questions and dialogue with the teachers. They were amazed at His understanding and His answers to their questions. Through this experience, He grew in favor with them. They thought highly of Him.

---

*F*inishing the process is everything to God.

Luke 2:52 concludes this story by stating, "And Jesus grew in wisdom and stature, and in favor with God and men" (*New International Version*).[26]

In your realm of experience—in your home, in your neighborhood, in your church, at your job—you should grow in wisdom and stature and in favor with God and men as well.

It's part of the process.

A classic biblical example of having favor is the Old Testament story of the widow whose husband's creditors were coming to take her sons because she had no money to pay the debts. As the story goes, she seeks out the Prophet Elisha for help:

> "The wife of a man from the company of the prophets cried out to Elisha, 'Your servant my husband is dead, and you know that he revered the Lord. But now his creditor is coming to take my two boys as his slaves.
>
> "Elisha replied to her, 'How can I help you? Tell me, what do you have in your house?'
>
> "'Your servant has nothing there at all,' she said, 'except a little oil' (2 Kings 4:1-2, *New International Version*).[27]

Elisha then instructs the widow to borrow all the vessels she can from her neighbors—not "neighbor" but neighbors. He didn't want her to borrow just a few vessels. He wanted her to get a whole bunch.

So she went from house to house borrowing all the vessels she could.

Obviously, she wasn't one of those grumpy neighbors no one likes, because her neighbors did give her vessels. She couldn't have been one that never did anything for anyone, always complained, gossiped or just let her trash blow all over their lawns.

Favor with her neighbors was a critical factor in the success of this venture. If she hadn't had favor with them, Elisha's plan would have never worked, and the widow's sons would have been taken by her late husband's creditors.

Once she was finished gathering vessels, Elisha told her to get in the house and begin pouring the little oil she had into the vessels...and to just keep pouring.

She did until she filled all the vessels.

When she needed favor from God, because she had treated people in a way pleasing to God, she got what she needed—and more!

Then Elisha instructed her, "Sell all the oil, pay your debts, live off the rest" (verse 7).[27]

I guarantee you that she sold all that oil because she had favor. She had favor in her community. And when she needed favor from God, because she had treated people in a way pleasing to God, she got what she needed—and more! She was able to pay all the debts, and she and her sons were able to live off the rest. God didn't just meet her need—He blessed her with more than enough with plenty left over. That's the kind of God He is—and He'll be that kind of God to you if you'll go through the process that leads to accruing wealth no matter how long it takes.

CHAPTER 4
Faithfulness– It Expedites the Process

In Genesis 12:2, God made a promise to Abraham— and to every believer thereafter including you and me—that we would be exceedingly fruitful in whatever we did. Then He added, "You shall be a blessing" (*New King James Version*).[28]

If you have more than enough with plenty left over, then you have become a blessing.

If you have more than enough with plenty left over in your marriage, then you are able to help others in their marriages. You are able to share wisdom and understanding with other couples who need help and encouragement.

Having more than enough with plenty left over isn't just about finances. It's about every area of your life. It's about the entire spectrum of your life having more than enough joy with plenty left over...more than enough hope, peace, healing, contentment, humility, self-control...and every attribute God has empowered a Christian to have.

Imagine having more than enough patience with plenty left over?! I know there have been times in my life when I really needed that—like on shopping trips with my wife. There have been times when it was supposed to be a shopping trip for me...what I call a "Jack Day." On those days, we shop for whatever it is that I need.

I remember one trip when we were looking for a new suit for me, and she asked, "Do you mind if I go in this one store and look?"

"Of course, not," I smiled lovingly. "No problem, Honey."

I really didn't mind, but when she'd been in there a while, I started getting impatient. I started getting cranky. I started getting down right impatient!

I needed more than enough with plenty left over!

Having more than enough with plenty left over is living a life of overflow.

But too many believers get sidetracked. They never make it to this place of abundance. They're like Joyce and I were when driving on the freeway one time. We had gone to dinner with friends, and when we left the restaurant, we took our typical route home. But when we attempted to get on the freeway, the entrance ramp was closed. So as I tried to find an alternate route, I got on the wrong entrance to the interstate and ended up having to drive way out to a mall, exit the highway, turn around and get back on going in the right direction.

In the same way, many believers spend way too many years trying to get turned around. They never reach more than enough with plenty left over because they are always in the process of trying to get turned around.

God is giving you the opportunity today to once and for all get your life straightened out and headed in the right direction. He's filled this book with direction and instruction to help you get on course and stay the course.

God wants us all steady on the right course.

Start With What You Have—And Make It Grow

Part of staying on the right course—once you're on it—is to remain faithful. Faithfulness can save you years in the process of accruing more than enough with plenty left over. It will protect you from mistakes and keep you on the right course for your life.

Faithfulness can save you years in the process of accruing more than enough with plenty left over. It will protect you from mistakes and keep you on the right course for your life.

Jesus taught an excellent parable about faithfulness when He told the story of the master who gave three servants different amounts of money. What each of those three servants did with the money is what we're to observe and learn from.

Matthew 25:14 begins this insightful story:

> "For the kingdom of heaven is like a man traveling to a far country, who called his own servants and delivered his goods to them.
>
> And to one he gave five talents, to another two, and to another one, to each according to his own ability; and immediately he went on a journey.
>
> Then he who had received the five talents went and traded with them, and made another five talents.
>
> And likewise he who had received two gained two more also.
>
> But he who had received one went and dug in the ground, and hid his lord's money" (Matthew 25:14-18, *New King James Version*).[29]

The original Greek meaning of the word *talents* is defined as about 75.6 pounds of gold. I find this interesting because Jesus could have told this story many ways, but He purposely chose to use a heavy level of money because He wanted to describe what all a believer can do if he is faithful with the resources God gives him.

He purposely chose to use a heavy level of money because He wanted to describe what all a believer can do if he is faithful with the resources God gives him.

When Jesus taught this parable, there were only two classes of people in the culture of the day. There were the very rich and the very poor. There was no middle class as we have in America. So the fact He used such large amounts to make His point is even more significant. He was really stretching their thinking—and ours.

For example, at the time of writing this book in 2005, the five talents would be worth more than a million dollars—$1,927,800 to be exact. The two talents would be worth $771,120, and the one talent would be equal to $385,560. That's a lot of money!

What amplifies the magnitude of the money is the understanding that because there were only two classes in Jesus' day—the very rich and the very poor—the money is worth even more.

In other words, if you took today's money equivalents, and rather than see it through the eyes of middle class America, you perceived it through the eyes of someone living in a third world country, even the servant with one talent worth $385,560 would be like a millionaire.

When I first considered such exchange rates, I thought, *Lord, they probably accused you of preaching on prosperity!*

Seriously, I think Jesus was trying to get across to those people and to us that He really does want us to have more than enough with plenty left over.

So why is all this money value and perception important?

Why did Jesus pick such extravagant amounts of money in His illustration?

What was His point?

First, Jesus wanted to impress upon their minds the importance of being faithful with the resources God gives.

Second, He wanted them to know that God wants us all to always have more than enough with plenty left over. God will give us all the resources we need, not just to get by, but to get blessed…not just to pay a few bills off, but to be blessed to overflowing so you can be a blessing to others and give to every good work as the Holy Spirit leads you. God wants your marriage blessed to overflowing, your children blessed to overflowing, your entire life blessed to overflowing.

When we can think like God thinks, we'll realize that nothing is impossible. We'll not reason and rationalize away what God wants to accomplish through and for us.

Too often, probably like the people listening to Jesus that day, we are limited in our thinking. But Jesus isn't. He thinks much bigger—about everything, including money.

Which Servant Are You?

Matthew 25:19-29 goes on to say:

> After a long time the lord of those servants came and settled accounts with them.
>
> So he who had received five talents came and brought five other talents, saying, "Lord, you delivered to me five talents; look, I have gained five more talents besides them."
>
> His lord said to him, "Well done, good and faithful servant; you were faithful over a few things, I will make you ruler over many things. Enter into the joy of your lord."

He also who had received two talents came and said, "Lord, you delivered to me two talents; look, I have gained two more talents besides them."

His Lord said to him, "Well done, good and faithful servant; you have been faithful over a few things, I will make you ruler over many things. Enter into the joy of your lord."

Then he who had received the one talent came and said, "Lord, I knew you to be a hard man, reaping where you have not sown, and gathering where you have not scattered seed. And I was afraid, and went and hid your talent in the ground. Look, there you have what is yours." But his lord answered and said to him, "You wicked and lazy servant, you knew that I reap where I have not sown, and gather where I have not scattered seed. So you ought to have deposited my money with the bankers, and at my coming I would have received back my own with interest. So take the talent from him, and give it to him who has ten talents.

For to everyone who has, more will be given, and he will have abundance; but from him who does not have, even what he has will be taken away. And cast the unprofitable servant into the outer darkness. There will be weeping and gnashing of teeth."[30]

I find each of these servants interesting and unique. I think they are examples that   reveal the different ways of how we might be and how we want to be.

For example, the servant who was given five talents doubled his resources. He initiated action without being asked. He saw what needed to be done and he did it. He had an attitude of going the extra mile and it took him to greater heights.

You can be like this servant! You can develop an initiator way of living, his attitude of going the extra mile takes him to greater heights. You can initiate positive behaviors in your marriage, in your family, at work or church. You can be the one who sees a piece of paper on the ground and takes the initiative by picking it up—rather than thinking someone else will get it.

> *You can develop an initiator way of living.*

If you'll become the initiator, then you will become the ultimate faithful believer and you will see increase more in your life than you could ever imagine. It will manifest in every area of your life—from home to work to the world.

The third servant, who was separated from God because he hid his talent and did nothing with it, represents the kind of person who makes up excuses for why he can't do what he's asked.

Personally, I want to be like the first servant who had five talents. It was he and the second servant that God called faithful—and it is the faithful who will be blessed with having more than enough with plenty left over.

The Fruit of Faithfulness

Faithfulness—the genuine, heartfelt, genuine kind—is having a consistency in the things that God uses to bring forth fruit.

Proverbs 28:20 says: "A faithful man will abound with blessings, but he who hastens to be rich will not go unpunished" (*New King James Version*).[31]

The faithful man, the person who is consistent in doing the Word of God, who won't sacrifice his ethics will abound with blessings. Abound means having more than you need. It's a constant flow of something.

Therefore, the faithful man will have a constant flow of increase coming into his life. His life will be as Deuteronomy 28:2 says, "All these blessings will come upon you and overtake you if you obey the LORD your God" (*New American Standard Version*).[32] In other words, the blessings will track you down. They'll hunt you down!

The faithful man, the person who is consistent in doing the Word of God, who won't sacrifice his ethics will abound with blessings.

On the other hand, the person who tries to take a shortcut to wealth, or a shortcut to success, will reap some kind of harm on the journey. The shortcut will cost him something he doesn't want to pay.

Being faithful isn't just doing the same thing. It's doing what He says that will make your marriage better, or that will improve your finances, or that will give you peace in the midst of a storm.

Faithfulness is consistently doing the work, and consistently doing it to the point that it brings forth fruit. In other words, there is an aspect of faithfulness that we can't lose sight of and that is completion. Faithfulness is doing the job and then finishing the job. It's starting the process, and finishing the process.

I remember as a kid when I'd do my chores. If I didn't complete them, I wasn't considered faithful. To be considered faithful, I had to do the task the way my parents said, and I had to complete the task. If I took the garbage out but missed the pickup day, I wasn't faithful, because I didn't do the task properly. I messed up.

Life is the same way. To be faithful on the job, we have to start our assignments and complete them.

It's not enough to start the process of anything and not finish.

We can't start going to church, and then quit.

We can't start the process of prayer, and then quit.

We can't start the process of worshipping God from our hearts, developing intimacy with Him and then quit.

It's simply not enough. We have to continue the processes in our lives to the point that we bear fruit. Then we are truly faithful.

Faithfulness is the character of God. God is faithful to the point He bears fruit. When we manifest His character in our lives, He more than willingly gives us more than enough with plenty left over. He gives to us when He sees us practicing His Word and bearing fruit.

A lighthearted—but very real—example of faithfulness that you men can test on your wives is this: Every day tell her at least 15 times that you love her. Tell her when you wake up, while you're getting ready, at breakfast, before you leave, when you're leaving, later on the phone...and so on. Say, "Honey, I just wanted to tell you that I love you."

Then watch what happens.

She won't be asking, "Do you love me?"

And you won't have to be answering, "Of course, I love you. I told you 20 years ago when we married."

Consistency—even in everyday things—bears fruit!

If you are consistent in your parenting, in disciplining your children, then you will bear fruit—good fruit. Real faithfulness is more than just "showing up." It's going the distance to get a result.

Faithfulness Is Not An Option

Faithfulness is an ongoing state of a person who is continuously practicing what he has learned and is continually producing fruit. A faithful man is someone who is constantly practicing what produces much fruit in his life—in season after season. He's just as committed to God in the summer time as he is in the winter time. He's just as committed to God when the playoffs are happening, as when they're not. He's just as committed to God when Christmas season comes, as he is the rest of the year.

> *Real faithfulness is more than just "showing up." It's going the distance to get a result.*

Many people proclaim they are faithful, but we all need to self-evaluate from time to time to make sure we're on the right track. Proverbs 20:6 says, "Most men will proclaim each his own goodness, but who can find a faithful man?" (*New King James Version*).[33]

The essence of this verse is that true faithfulness is a rarity. It's not something everyone has, because it requires that you continually do it—even when you don't feel like it. It requires that you be faithful when no one else is being faithful.

This is against our human nature. We tend to go with the flow, join the majority or be a part of the crowd. But a faithful man isn't like that. He doesn't just pray because the leadership at the church has declared a "season of prayer." No. He prays all the time. He still forgives, even when the pastor isn't preaching on forgiveness. He still lives right, even when there are no reminders of morality.

First Corinthians 4:2 says, "Moreover it is required in stewards that one be found faithful" (*New King James Version*).[34]

Faithfulness is not an option. It's a requirement—if you want more than enough with plenty left over. It's what it takes to reap a harvest of abundance in every area of your life.

Fish Won't Just Jump In The Boat!

Whether you are a fisherman or not, you and I both know that fishing requires faithfulness because fish have a mind of their own. They do not just jump in the boat. Unless you throw a stick of dynamite into the water and blow them up and out of the water, the only legitimate way to get fish out of the water and into the boat is to go fishing—and fishing requires a lot of diligence and patience.

First, you have to get up in the wee hours of the morning—because for some reason fish won't bite when we're all awake and alert—then you have to use the right bait, and lastly, you have to be willing to sit there until you catch one.

That last step is the proving ground. That's where your real faithfulness to fishing shows up. I've known people who have fished for steelhead for four or five years and never caught one—yet they keep going back.

Talk about faithfulness!

We have to be that faithful—that consistent—when it comes to loving our husband or wife, loving our children, loving our country, our neighbors and our church families.

Relationship with your husband or wife isn't going to jump in the boat.

Prosperity isn't going to jump into your boat.

Healing isn't going to jump into your boat.

Nothing will.

But faithfulness—taking action—will get what you want into your boat. Determine to be faithful—to consistently do whatever is required of you until you produce fruit. Be like the servant with the five talents. Take the initiative. Be the first one in your marriage to make changes. Be the first one to be more responsible concerning money, being balanced or expressing love. If you will, you will have more than enough with plenty left over in that area of your life— and the best part is you will have enough left over for others.

Remember what Jesus said to the servant with the five talents. "You were faithful over a few things, I will make you ruler over many things. Enter into the joy of your Lord."

Jesus called $1,927,800 "a few things." The *King James Version* translates it "little." The servant was faithful with the multimillions God allowed to come into his hands and God called it "little!"

---

*F*aithfulness is how you can speed up the process in your life of getting from where you are to where you want to be

---

Do you see God's perspective? He calls millions "being faithful over little."

If you're like me, when I saw this, my mental furniture was all rearranged! God knows how to renew our minds, doesn't He?

If you want more—in any area of your life—then be faithful. Faithfulness is how you can speed up the process in your life of getting from where you are to where you want to be—living life with more than enough with plenty left over.

Chapter 5

How God Rewards You

When I was a kid, my parents always provided clothes for me. They provided a bed for me. They provided food for me. I always ate breakfast, lunch and supper. They were good parents and ensured that all my basic needs were met.

But when it was my birthday, they rewarded me.

When it was Christmas, they rewarded me.

Like any kid, I knew the difference between basic needs and rewards. Rewards are when you get what you really want.

I can remember my mom and dad asking me on Christmas Day, "Did you get everything you wanted?"

They loved me and enjoyed rewarding me. I was the same way raising our children. I was always eager to know if they had gotten everything they really wanted for Christmas.

In our adult lives, I liken it to paying bills. You have to have money for the electricity, the water and the mortgage. There's no thrill in sending the mortgage payment. But having money for a great vacation, now, that's a reward.

For most people a basic car is a necessity. But a two-seater Mercedes convertible is a reward.

It's good to have enough clothes, but even better to go shopping and buy all the suits or dresses you want without looking at the price tags. That's a reward shopping trip!

Rewards are important. They are the "plenty left over" we all want.

Hebrews 11:6 reveals how God is more than willing to reward us: "But without faith it is impossible to please Him, for he who comes to God must believe that He is, and that He is a rewarder of those who diligently seek Him" *(New King James Version)*.[35]

In this verse, it is clear that God is a rewarder, not just someone who meets our needs. He's telling us that if we want to have more than enough with plenty left over in our marriages or finances, that if we'll diligently seek Him concerning those areas, then He will do far more than just meet our requests. He will reward us in our marriages, and reward us in our finances.

So how do you diligently seek God? *Diligence* means "a constant consistency in something." To diligently seek God is to have a constant consistency in your relationship with Him—to be consistent in your intimate fellowship with Him. It's gearing your entire life around getting to know Him better.

Sounds like faithfulness doesn't it?

Psalm 34:10 says, "But those who seek the LORD shall not lack any good thing" (*New King James Version*).[36] Those who continually seek to know Him better and better and better are the ones whom He will reward.

We're to seek God out of love for Him, and in return, as an expression of His love for us, He pours out the blessings in our lives.

In fact, the Bible says God will give you all the things you desire, all the things you ever wanted, if you make Him your central purpose (Psalm 37:4;[37] John 15:7).[38]

God's prosperity, His willingness to give us the desires of our hearts, is not about acquiring things. We are not to seek God to get things.

We're to seek God out of love for Him, and in return, as an expression of His love for us, He pours out the blessings in our lives.

Increase Your Affection

If you're struggling with faithfulness, I have a simple assignment that will help you: Be more affectionate.

For example, if you want your marriage to be better, the first step is not to sort through all of your problems. I believe you should simply go out and have a good time.

"Well, I don't want to be with him" you may say.

That's the problem you need to overcome. You need to increase in your affection toward him. You can't begin to solve your marital problems unless you are faithful toward him (or her), and you can't be faithful toward anything you don't have a strong affection for.

If you are a parent with a challenging teen, become affectionate toward him or her. I've known parents who have basically written off their children because they've given them such a hard time. Those parents quit. They lost their affection.

A faithful man or woman can't do that.

Many people quit in ministry because they lose their affection for it.

As soon as someone loses his or her affection for something, they stop being faithful. Stay passionate toward everything you do...toward your job, your spouse, your children.

If you just don't like your job, then get passionate toward your paycheck! Get passionate toward your job because it is a stepping-stone to a better job.

Do your job according to Ephesians 6:5-8, knowing that as you do your job as unto the Lord a better one will come along: "Servants, be obedient to them that are your masters [bosses] according to the flesh, with fear and trembling, in singleness of your heart, as unto Christ; Not with eyeservice, as menpleasers; but as the servants of Christ, doing the will of God from the heart; With good will doing service, *as to the Lord, and not to men:* Knowing that whatsoever good thing any man doeth, *the same shall he receive of the Lord,* whether he be bond or free" (*King James Version,* emphasis mine).[39]

If you'll be passionate and affectionate, you'll abound with blessings. God will reward you. All you have to do is be faithful to do whatever God's Word says until the reward begins to happen in your life. Jesus spoke of this when He told the parable of the barren fig tree:

> A certain man had a fig tree planted in his vineyard, and he came seeking fruit on it and found none.
>
> Then he said to the keeper of his vineyard, "Look, for three years I have come seeking fruit on this fig tree and find none. Cut it down; why does it use up the ground?"
>
> But he answered and said to him, "Sir, let it alone this year also, until I dig around it and fertilize it. And if it bears fruit, well. But if not, after that you can cut it down" (Luke 13:6-9, *New King James Version*).[40]

A fig tree takes approximately 3 years before a farmer can expect figs. Based on that calculation, we can ascertain that the tree in the parable had been in the ground for six years—and still hadn't produced any fruit.

Yet the gardener says, "Give me one more chance with it. Let me dig around it a little bit here and fertilize it." He's affectionate toward the tree he's tended for so long.

Being faithful is staying with something until you produce results, until you produce fruit. It's keeping your affection alive toward something.

Staying faithful until you produce fruit was a very serious subject to Jesus. In the parable of the vine, He spoke about people who didn't produce fruit. He compared them to vines that are pruned, and any vine that doesn't produce fruit is cut off, its branches gathered, and then it is burned.

> I am the vine; you are the branches. If a man remains in me and I in him, he will bear much fruit; apart from me you can do nothing. If anyone does not remain in me, he is like a branch that is thrown away and withers; such branches are picked up, thrown into the fire and burned. If you remain in me and my words remain in you, ask whatever you wish, and it will be given you. This is to my Father's glory, that you bear much fruit, showing yourselves to be my disciples (John 15:5-8, *New International Version*).[41]

God will reward you if you are faithful, if you stay with something until it bears good fruit. First Corinthians 3:10-15 says:

> By the grace God has given me, I laid a foundation as an expert builder, and someone else is building on it. But each one should be careful how he builds. For no one can lay any foundation other than the one already laid, which is Jesus Christ. If any man builds on this foundation using gold, silver, costly stones, wood, hay or straw, his work will be shown for what it is, because the Day will bring it to light. It will be revealed with fire, and the fire

will test the quality of each man's work. If what he has built survives, *he will receive his reward*. If it is burned up, he will suffer loss; he himself will be saved, but only as one escaping through the flames *(New International Version)*. [42]

God Wants to Reward You Now

There is an illusion in the Body of Christ today about fruitfulness. Too many believers think that it doesn't really matter if we bear fruit here on earth. But the Bible doesn't teach that. God doesn't teach that.

God says He rewards your faithfulness right here on earth, right now.

I've heard many believers say, "Well the Lord told me to do this," but what they are doing is not bearing fruit. They'll spend five, 10, or 20 years doing something that bears no fruit.

God says He rewards your faithfulness right here on earth, right now.

God wouldn't have told them to do that. They are following a dream God really didn't birth, and they've spiritualized it.

The truth is God will only tell you to do things that bear much fruit. God will only tell you to do things that will work out in your life.

This is true on a grand scale and in the small events of daily life. For example, if I don't do what the Word says, my wife and I won't have a good relationship. I've got to love her the right way, help her in raising our children, be positive toward her, be encouraging to her—and do it HERE, not in the sweet by and by.

> *Life in God is all about the here and now. There has to be a consistent flow of practicing the aspects of God's Word so that we can bear much fruit.*

Life in God is all about the here and now. There has to be a consistent flow of practicing the aspects of God's Word so that we can bear much fruit.

Imagine the degree to which you could alter your life by becoming the most positive person you could be for the rest of your life. You would totally change everything because you would no longer have those self-fulfilled prophecies fulfilled by your negativity.

> *If you'll become affectionate to the things of God, you will increase your faithfulness—and if you are faithful, then you will bear much fruit. You will be rewarded right here, right now.*

"It's going to be one of those days." Yes it is, because you declared it and then you attracted the negativity. Trouble came looking for you—and found you.

But if you'll be positive, you'll attract what is positive. You'll attract vision, opportunities and answers. You'll attract happiness—and you'll repel grumpy, grumpy, grumpy!

If you'll become affectionate to the things of God, you will increase your faithfulness—and if you are faithful, then you will bear much fruit. You will be rewarded right here, right now.

Succeeding At Faithfulness & Getting the Rewards

While a great attitude and strong determination will take you far, you need more. You cannot succeed at faithfulness without the knowledge of success—because you have to practice enough of any activity that produces results. You have to have the knowledge of success that the Word of God gives.

For example, it is recorded in Acts 20:35 what the Apostle Paul said as he was leaving one of the churches he had started. He was referencing something Jesus told him: "In everything I did, I showed you that by this kind of hard work we must help the weak, remembering the words the Lord Jesus himself said: 'It is more blessed to give than to receive'" (*New International Version*).[43]

The reason it is more blessed to give than to receive is whenever I'm giving, serving or encouraging, I am sowing seeds into the ground of my life, and they will come up later in the next season of life and produce a bountiful harvest.

The act of giving produces blessing in your life—health, healing, finances, peace, restored relationships and so on.

This is knowledge you need in order to succeed.

Giving is priming the pump. So don't eat all your seed. You'll just starve the next harvest. Share your seed. Sow it, and the more you sow the more harvest you'll have.

Teach your children to live this way as well. If you will, one day they may knock on your door and say, "Dad, I just wanted to say thank you. God prospered me so much I bought you a new BMW!"

If you don't teach them, they'll knock on your door and say, "Can we move in for awhile? We're broke!" Then they'll sit around and watch TV and spill popcorn all over your sofa...just like they did when they were kids!

Give them what they need to be successful so they can grow up and continue to be a blessing. Model it before them day and night. Model faithfulness that produces more than enough with plenty left over.

The Apostle John wrote: "This is the confidence we have in approaching God: that if we ask anything *according to his will*, he hears us. And if we know that he hears us–whatever we ask–we know that we have what we asked of him" (1 John 5:14-15, *New International Version*).[44]

Asking according to His will is asking in agreement with what God's Word says, and what He has led you to do in your life. So if God says to you, "Listen, I want to give you a ride to success every day. I'll pick you up down the street on the corner at 6 a.m. in the morning," and you respond, "Yes, Lord. I agree with that! I'm all for it. I'll be there," then you are in agreement.

To fulfill your agreement, there will be some things required of you. You'll have to get up at 5 a.m. and shower. You'll have to get dressed, eat breakfast and get to the corner by 6 a.m. That's your part in the agreement.

God will always be faithful. If He said He'd be at the corner at 6 a.m., you can bank on it that He'll be there. But you won't benefit from His faithfulness if you don't show up on time. You have to keep your part of the agreement.

Too often, we say "I agree" to something we read in God's Word, or to something we hear from Him, but we aren't faithful, and so we don't benefit from His faithfulness.

Stay faithful to what you have agreed with.

If you are born again, you agreed He is Lord. You agreed He would call the shots in your life. You agreed you would raise up your children in the Lord. You agreed you would love your wife as Christ loved the church. You agreed you would submit to, respect and honor your husband.

Be faithful so you can receive the benefits of God's faithfulness to you.

I know I've not been faithful at times. It takes diligence and determination. I know I've said, "Yes, Lord. You said in Your Word to believe and receive, so I do. I'll be faithful," and I'll do great for a season. But when something comes up, I forget and start saying something different than what I'm believing. So I never make it to the destination of where God's faithfulness and my faithfulness cause His will to come to pass in my life.

It's like saying, "I believe I receive my healing," and two hours later you say, "I hope God heals me someday."

Five hours later you say, "I hope God just sovereignly heals me."

---

*M*ake up your mind to agree with His Word and remain faithful.

Eight hours later you say, "I hope the pastor gets a Word and calls out my sickness in the Sunday night service."

Make up your mind to agree with His Word and remain faithful. If you stay with it—whatever it is in your life today—you'll reap results. You'll reap the consequences of faithfulness—much fruit, and with much fruit comes great rewards.

CHAPTER 6

God Wants You to Have Quality *and* Quantity

When Moses and the children of Israel reached the edge of The Promised Land (Canaan), Moses sent 10 spies to check it out. He sent them all over the land to survey it and bring back a report.

When they returned, along with their report, they brought back some fruit. Numbers 13:23-24 says, "When they reached the Valley of Eshcol, they cut off a branch bearing a single cluster of grapes. Two of them carried it on a pole between them, along with some pomegranates and figs. That place was called the Valley of Eshcol because of the cluster of grapes the Israelites cut off there" (*New International Version*).[45]

The significance of this verse is that the fruitfulness in The Promised Land was much more than we realize. It took two men to carry the cluster of grapes on a pole, along with some pomegranates and figs. Even today in Eshcol there still grows huge clusters of grapes—grapes the size of plums.

When God told Moses and the children of Israel that He wanted to bring them into this land flowing with milk and honey, He was not only talking about the *quantity* of the surplus the land had to offer, but also He was talking about the *quality* of the surplus in Canaan.

God always wants you to have what you need with a surplus of quantity *and* quality. He wants the absolute very best for you. He loves you! He wants you to have more than enough with plenty left over!

> God always wants to give you more, but not just more of any old quality. He wants to give you the best of the best.

This principle of God's character is evident over and over in the Bible...from the grapes in the land of Canaan to the Wedding in Cana where Jesus turned water into the finest wine ever. God always wants to give you more, but not just more of any old quality. He wants to give you the best of the best.

John 2:4 begins the story of Jesus turning the water into wine.

On the third day a wedding took place at Cana in Galilee. Jesus' mother was there, and Jesus and his disciples had also been invited to the wedding.

When the wine was gone, Jesus' mother said to him, "They have no more wine."

"Dear woman, why do you involve me?" Jesus replied, "My time has not yet come."

His mother said to the servants, "Do whatever he tells you." Nearby stood six stone water jars, the kind used by the Jews for ceremonial washing, each holding from twenty to thirty gallons. Jesus said to the servants, "Fill the jars with water"; so they filled them to the brim. Then he told them, "Now draw some out and take it to the master of the banquet."

They did so, and the master of the banquet tasted the water that had been turned into wine. He did not realize where it had come from, though the servants who had drawn the water knew. Then he called the bridegroom aside and said, "Everyone brings out the choice wine first and then the cheaper wine after the guests have had too much to drink; but you have saved the best till now" (*New International Version*).[46]

There are two critical points we need to see in this account. First, the quantity that Jesus provided. There were six pots holding anywhere from 25-30 gallons. Now, I like to have thorough understanding of such details, so I researched equivalents for those pots. I read, for example, that a keg of beer holds 31 gallons. So these six pots were very close in volume to six kegs.

So this wedding reception was a really big party, and the pots were empty!

So Jesus performs a miracle and refills the pots. Now keep in mind, despite how humorous it is that these pots were the size of modern-day kegs, that wine in Jesus' day was very weak and everyone drank it as a daily beverage. It would make today's wine seem like hard liquor. Everyone drank grape juice in His day…keeping it in a paste, mixing it with water and making wine out of it.

So Jesus wasn't helping everyone get snockered! He was replenishing what everyone drank all the time—a very low-alcoholic content wine.

Jesus made a tremendous quantity for the reception. He made more than enough with plenty left over.

But notice what the host says to the bridegroom after tasting it: "Everyone brings out the choice wine first and then the cheaper wine after the guests have had too much to drink; but you have saved the best till now" (*New International Version*).[46]

The second point is the quality that Jesus provided. The wine Jesus made was the best. It was better than anything the world had to offer at the time. He didn't make a quality that would just get by. That's not God's way. God never gives us just enough to get by. He always does the outstanding in our lives. He gives us quantity AND quality. He gives us quality in our marriages, in our health, in our families, in our jobs, in our finances…in every area.

Taste and See

God wants you to develop a taste, an appetite for quality. He created you to desire the best and to receive the best.

Psalm 34:8 and 10 confirm this saying, "Oh taste and see that the Lord is good...those that seek the Lord shall not lack any good thing" (*New King James Version*).[47]

> *God wants you to develop a taste, an appetite for quality. He created you to desire the best and to receive the best.*

The word *see* in this verse means "to perceive." God wants His people to not only develop a taste for excellence, but He wants them to have an eye for excellence as well. That's why He says, "If you seek the Lord, you shall not lack any good thing."

It's very easy to become accustomed to living a life that is far below your spiritual potential. It's easy to contaminate our lives by watching the wrong things on television, or putting the wrong food and drinks into our bodies. It's easy to live careless lives and think *I'm normal.*

> *God wants His people to not only develop a taste for excellence, but He wants them to have an eye for excellence as well.*

No. Living this way—and many other careless ways—is living way below your spiritual potential. You don't have to live bound to any bad habits. You don't have to live bound by any addictions. You don't have to live in a constant state of upheaval or crisis.

You were born—again—free. You are a child of God. God wants to train you to reign. You were born to live the life of a free person, not a slave. Yet, many people live enslaved to wrong thinking and settle for a life of so much less than God wants them to have.

They think on what they need today, on instant gratification. God wants us all to think of our future, and provide for it.

Don't think the minimum in life, think the maximum. Develop an eye for excellence in raising your children, in what you do with your skills and talents. Acquire a taste for quality.

I've mentioned this before, but I like to make lattes for my wife, Joyce. When I first learned to make a latte, I went around town to about ten different places and asked them how they made their drinks. I inquired about everything—from what syrups they used to temperature settings to ingredients. I wanted to make a great latte.

So I began working on my latte-making at home.

Despite all my effort, something was lacking in the quality of my home-made latte compared to the coffee houses.

Well, one day Joyce brought home a bag of fresh-ground coffee, so fresh, it was still warm. I instantly made us both a latte. It was so much better with freshly ground beans! We were so impressed by the difference that I never make a latte now without first grinding my own beans.

That's how every area of our lives should be. We should keep stretching and searching for what's best. God doesn't want us to become accustomed to living at a lower moral standard. He doesn't want us living expecting a certain level of discipline from our children that is far too low. He doesn't want them swinging from the chandeliers and jumping on the couch! It's not normal to let your children run wild. It's not normal to live addicted. It's not normal to live immorally. It's not normal to live below God's level of excellence.

Taste and see that the Lord is good! God wants you to develop an eye for excellence in your trade, your skill, the way you keep house, the way you treat your family members and other people. God has called you to excellence, not sloppiness.

I love the way my wife takes the time to fix herself up, even on days when we don't go out and it's just the two of us at home. She does that for me, because she loves me...but also because she has an eye for excellence.

God wants us to live above "just getting by." Just getting by is living "that close" to having an affair, or "that close" to your kids being on drugs. Sure, you may be doing great in comparison to a lot of other people, but go for the best. Go for God's excellence.

Discipline yourself by practicing on those things that may not seem like they matter—even though they do. Practice on how you keep up your car, your appearance, your home, and so on. Dare yourself to live differently than everyone around you.

I remember when the United States was publicly moving toward war with Iraq after 9-11. President Bush and England's Prime Minister Tony Blair were standing on what they believed was right, while the popular vote was against them. But they stood.

You are to stand as well. Don't take the easy way or the path of least resistance. Take the most excellent way.

Proverbs 28:20 says a faithful person will abound with blessings.[48] Abound means to have more than enough, like the constant flow of a river. When you have an eye for excellence, the blessings will be constantly flowing in your life.

A bound means to have more than enough, like the constant flow of a river. When you have an eye for excellence, the blessings will be constantly flowing in your life.

Add to Your Faith

Whatever you have prayed for and are believing for, if you'll add a taste and eye for excellence to your life, your faith will be more effective.

Second Peter 1:5 says, "Add to your faith virtue,"[49] which also translates as "excellence." In other words, God is instructing us to: "With great diligence, add to your faith excellence." You are only able to do that as you acquire a taste for excellence.

When you have an eye for excellence and you are believing for things with excellence, your faith will be more effective.

James 5:17 says, "Elijah was a man just like us. He prayed earnestly that it would not rain, and it did not rain on the land for three and a half years" (*New International Version*).[50]

Elijah had an eye for excellence, because he didn't just pray it wouldn't rain. There was no moisture of any kind for 3 ½ years…no dew, nothing.

When you have an eye for excellence, you can pray fervently and receive your answers. "The effective, fervent prayer of a righteous man avails much" (James 5:16, *New King James Version*).[51]

Think about this. If you are praying for transportation, are you thinking about an old clunker, or have you really put some thought into what you need and want? Do you need a family vehicle? A van? Do you know what is safest and financially a sound move?

When you take these kinds of steps, then when you pray, there will be fervency in your prayers. That's adding to your faith, excellence.

The same is true if you are believing for a house. Do you just want a roof, any old roof, over your head? If so, there are barns aplenty in this country.

What do you and your family really need and really want? Do you need to live close to your job? Which school district do you want to live in? How about believing for a laundry room that really is a room?!

Fervency. Excellence. God wants you to be specific. He wants you to have an eye for excellence so that you can have more than enough with plenty left over.

James also says, "Faith without works is dead" (James 2:26).[52] It is not enough to believe you receive. It's not enough to just pray. You have to put some action with your faith to make it work.

Putting Action With Your Faith

Putting action with your faith can be as simple as sowing seed—but it has to be the right seed.

---

*F*ervency. Excellence. God *wants you to be specific.*

For example, if you need $120,000, you can pray, ask God for it and proclaim, "I believe I receive."

But that's not enough. You need to sow seed.

The Bible says sowing seed leads to three primary levels of increase: reaping 30 times as much as you sow, reaping 60 times as much as you sow, and reaping 100 times as much as you sow. Jesus illustrated this principle through the parable of the sower:

> Then Jesus said to them, "Don't you understand this parable? How then will you understand any parable?
>
> The farmer sows the word. Some people are like seed along the path, where the word is sown. As soon as they hear it, Satan comes and takes away the word that was sown in them.
>
> Others, like seed sown on rocky places, hear the word and at once receive it with joy. But since they have no root, they last only a short time. When trouble or persecution comes because of the word, they quickly fall away.
>
> Still others, like seed sown among thorns, hear the word; but the worries of this life, the deceitfulness of wealth and the desires for other things come in and choke the word, making it unfruitful.

Others, like seed sown on good soil, hear the word, accept it, and produce a crop–thirty, sixty or even a hundred times what was sown" (Mark 4:13-20, *New International Version*).[53]

If I wanted to believe for a hundredfold return, for one hundred times what I sowed, then I would need to sow $1200. But let me warn you. One-hundredfold returns only come from sacrificial giving. Throughout the Bible when people receive great increase, it's usually because they sowed the most generous way they could.

> *Greater sacrifice will always result in a greater return when planted into good soil—if your heart is right.*

Greater sacrifice will always result in a greater return when planted into good soil—if your heart is right. On the other hand, less sacrifice will result in a smaller return.

"He who sows sparingly will also reap sparingly, and he who sows bountifully will also reap bountifully." (2 Corinthians 9:6 *New King James Version*).[54]

When God told Isaac to sow into the land of the Philistines, he reaped a hundredfold return in the same year.

To have more than enough with plenty left over in our lives, we will have to operate within the principles of God's Word. We will have to invest in the kingdom of heaven.

God will tell you what to sow and where to sow it. If He tells you a sacrificial amount, then give it, trusting Him to be faithful to His Word.

God Will Promote You to the Front of the Line

God wants to bring you up from the level you're living on to a higher level. It's a process...but if you'll remain faithful, you will reap the benefits of His faithfulness.

He wants to promote you in every area of your life, to move you from the back of the line to the front of the line, from living with too little to living with more than enough.

In Matthew 20, Jesus told the story of a landowner who hired several workers at different intervals throughout the day, but he paid them all the same at the end of the day, even though they didn't all put in a full day's work.

At the end of the parable in verse 16, Jesus gives us the point of the story: "So the last will be first, and the first will be last."[55]

If you are at the back of the line, God will bring you up to the front of the line! If you're going through life flying coach, God will bring you up front to fly first class. If you are at the back of your life, with everything going haywire, God wants to help you straighten out your life and get on the right track. If you are born again, everything you need pertaining to life and godliness is already on the inside of you (2 Peter 1:3).[56] Everything you need for your natural life, for your personal journey on this earth is already on the inside of you. You just need to learn how to tap into it.

Ephesians 1:3 assures us: "Blessed be the God and Father of our Lord Jesus Christ, who has blessed us with every spiritual blessing in the heavenly places in Christ" (*New King James Version*).[57]

Everything you need for your natural life, for your personal journey on this earth is already on the inside of you. You just need to learn how to tap into it.

In other words, God has placed His salvation inside of us. He has put healing inside of us. He has put prosperity inside of us. He's put success, deliverance and victory inside of us.

And you bring it out into the natural realm with your faith.

So you already have more than enough because you have Jesus.

You already have more than enough with plenty left over!

Pull Up a Chair

God has never intended for you to just shuffle through life, get by on leftovers and squeak through the pearly gates. There is nothing in His Word that indicates such a downtrodden life.

Quite the contrary, God wants you to have the best...and His Word reaffirms it over and over.

Psalm 23:4-6 says, "Yeh though I walk through the valley of the shadow of death, I will fear no evil; for you are with me; your rod and your staff they comfort me...You prepare a table before me in the presence of my enemies; You anoint my head with oil; My cup runs over. Surely goodness and mercy shall follow me all the days of my life; and I will dwell in the house of the Lord forever" (*New King James Version*).[58]

God has prepared a table for you. It's not a pauper's table, or a picnic table, or a beggar's table. God is a king and He has prepared a king's table for you.

So pull up a chair! Even though your life may feel like a wreck that just can't be repaired, God has the best in store for you. He has the table laid out with all the best silver, china and fancy dishes. He has the best food for you, delicacies you've never known.

God has prepared a table for you. It's not a pauper's table, or a picnic table, or a beggar's table. God is a king and He has prepared a king's table for you.

Even your cup runs over. It is filled to overflowing, never running empty. When this Psalm was written, the Jewish custom included making people feel welcome in their homes by keeping their cups full. But if they stayed too long, their cup wouldn't overflow anymore. Time to go home, Johnny!

But God never says it's time to go home. He says, "Your cup runs over." Forever. There will never be a dry time. There will never be a time when blessing isn't happening.

In God, there is a constant flow of more than enough with plenty left over—of both quantity and quality. God wants you to have the very best!

CHAPTER 7

Remember Where Your Wealth Comes From

The miracle at the Wedding in Cana was more than filling a supply need of good wine. It was a fore-shadowing of the future…all the way to the present age. The Bible says in John 2:11, "This beginning of *signs* Jesus did in Cana of Galilee, and manifested His glory; and His disciples believed in Him" (*New King James Version).*[59]

The miracle Jesus performed in Cana was a sign. A sign points to something down the road—just like a sign on the freeway points to what's coming up at the next exit. A sign tells you what is coming next so you can prepare for it.

The miracle Jesus performed in Cana points all the way to His Second Coming revealing what must take place before He comes. The miracle at Cana was a prototype of what all God has in store for us.

Simply put: The best is yet to come.

Remember when a taste of the new wine was taken to the master of the house? He was surprised that the bridegroom had saved the best for last.

That is a foreshadowing of our generation. We know from Bible prophecy that we are living in the end times—the season before the Second Coming of Jesus Christ. We are in the last days and God has saved the best for last.

We've seen the sign. Now it's time to prepare.

Rebuild & Restore

God is setting us up for some of the greatest days the history of the Church has ever seen. Like Israel in the Old Testament, we are in a preparation period.

Whenever Israel would sin (and lose everything) and then repent, they would have to reclaim The Promise Land. When they would retake possession of the land that flowed with milk and honey, and returned to Jerusalem, there would always be two assignments before them: rebuild and restore.

The Israelites would always have to rebuild the temple and restore the worship as it once had been.

In America today, we have to rebuild the walls of the temple, rebuild the inner sanctuary, and restore the true heart of worship and praise within the Church.

We've got to get real with God to receive the next outpouring of His Spirit. We've got to focus our hearts on Him with tremendous desire and passion. We've got to position ourselves to receive all that God is preparing.

In America today, we have to rebuild the walls of the temple, rebuild the inner sanctuary, and restore the true heart of worship and praise within the Church.

During the last decade, satan has put tremendous effort into neutralizing the praise and worship in the Church. Many musicians from international ministries have realized they've been caught up in an entertainment trap and have lost the anointing they once had. I've spoken to many professional Christian musicians and artists who have made similar confessions and observations. They've said comments like: "I was really into entertainment for a while. It seemed like that was the only way I could draw a crowd. But the Lord really dealt with me, and now I'm getting back into worship. I'm really getting back to heartfelt praise and acceleration toward God."

We've got to get real with God to receive the next outpouring of His Spirit. We've got to focus our hearts on Him with tremendous desire and passion. We've got to position ourselves to receive all that God is preparing.

77

The Holy Spirit has rushed into their lives and shown them His heart—and their hearts have turned back to what is pure and right. Consequently, the entire Church is getting back to something we lost. A byproduct of this move is that some of the greatest sales in CDs are worship CDs.

We're rebuilding and restoring on a worldwide Church level.

Where are you in this move of God?

Retrace Your Steps

Many believers—much like the Christian musicians and artists—have gotten away from worshipping from the heart. We've strayed from the right focus for our lives. It's time to retrace our steps.

I know at my house when I lose my keys, the first thing I do is retrace my tracks. I go back to where I think I had my keys last and then I start at that point and think, *Well, where would I have put them?*

Of course, I always check with my wife too, as she's always picking up and relocating my stuff! She likes to keep things nice and tidy...of course I love that about her...but it doesn't help me when I'm searching for my keys!

Some of us need to retrace our thoughts. We need to come back to the time when we used to worship and the presence of God filled our house to overflowing. We need to find the place where once again we say the name of "Jesus" and something tingles inside.

Go back to that place of getting up in the morning with a song in your heart.

Go back to that place of getting up in the morning with a song in your heart. Leave what's become dry Christianity in your life and find that fresh Christianity that's all about relationship—a relationship that fills your life with testimony after testimony.

Live in that place where you hear God all the time. Live in that place where praise and worship is alive in you and when you come to church you bring it with you. Then it hooks up with everyone else's fire and the place shakes with the power and presence of God!

Find that place! God is getting ready to pour out His Spirit like no other generation has ever seen, but if you are not in the right place, you won't experience it. If you are not ready spiritually, you won't be able to handle it.

As a Deer Pants, So Should You

When was the last time you thirsted and hungered after God? King David knew insatiable thirst. He wrote of it in Psalm 42.[60] At the time he was reaping destruction in every area. He had committed adultery with Bathsheba and murdered Uriah, her husband. His sin opened the door to Satan and his destruction. His son became rebellious and initiated an insurrection. David had to flee for his life and separate himself from the Ark of the Covenant which contained the presence of God in that age. (Today, the Spirit of God resides on the inside of us. We are the temple of the living God {1 Corinthians 3:16-17}.[61] But in David's day, God kept His presence in the Ark of the Covenant.)

So as the fugitive David longed for the presence of God, He wrote this Psalm expressing his dire thirst.

As the deer pants for the water brooks, so pants my soul for You, O God. My soul thirsts for God, for the living God. When shall I come and appear before God? My tears have been my food day and night, while they continually say to me, "Where is your God?" (Psalm 42:1-3, *New King James Version*).[60]

All of nature reveals the glory of God. The illustration of a deer is no coincidence. There is so much understanding to be gleaned from these verses simply by understanding the behaviors of deer.

For example, a male deer has antlers that cool his body, much like the radiator in a car. But a female deer—which is what David referenced—has an unquenchable thirst. She innately searches out water to quench her thirst.

If a deer is sick, he will begin to look for snake holes, even though the snake is a natural enemy of the deer. In fact, if you burn a deer's antlers, it will repel snakes.

Once a deer finds a snake hole, he will snort in the hole, forcing the fumes of his breath to drive out the snake. When the snake exits in self-defense, the deer will trample the snake and eat it. The poisonous venom of the snake inside the deer's body will produce tremendous thirst, so the deer will go to the nearest water source and drink enough water to dilute the poison as it goes throughout his or her body. Despite the poisonous nature of the venom, the deer knows it also is an antidote for what is ailing him.

Because of a deer's ability to care for itself, they have amazingly long lives. Alexander the Great put necklaces on deer that were found 100 years later.

Think about it. A deer knows that to survive it must put the serpent under its feet! A deer's antidote is putting to death the evil one.

That's what believers must do as well.

When you sense something is wrong, when something is missing inside, seek God. He'll reveal the serpent in your life. He'll reveal the evil in your life. Then you can breathe out of your mouth the Word of God. With repentance you can trample the evil. You can completely die to that issue in your life. And the desire of God will increase in your life once again.

Like the deer, you will pant for the water brooks of God.

When you sense something is wrong, when something is missing inside, seek God. He'll reveal the serpent in your life.

I believe God put the image of the deer and the snake in front of David and said, "David, you have sinned and you have repented. Now you can truly say that because you've treaded the serpent under your feet and confessed your sin with your mouth, that your hunger for Me is great. You are no longer sick in spirit. You are well."

When you are well, you desire the presence of God in your life.

Never Forget

Where are you in life? Is your relationship with God fresh? Or has it become "religiously stuffed?" When did it change? When you had a dispute with someone? When you gained a new friend? When you gained money and influence?

David never forgot the grace and forgiveness God extended to him. He went on to say in Psalm 84:10: "Better is one day in your courts than a thousand elsewhere; I would rather be a doorkeeper in the house of my God than dwell in the tents of the wicked" (*New International Version*).[62]

David was a multimillionaire when he wrote these words. He could have gone anywhere in the known world that he wanted. He had influence in the corner of every kingdom. There was nothing he couldn't do, buy or get. But he desired above all things to be with God.

As we approach the end-time outpouring of God, and the blessings begin to fill our lives, and we go from nothing to something, will we still thirst and hunger after God? Will you?

We can't afford to lose our desire for God. We can't afford to ever forget where our wealth really comes from.

I am a very blessed man. I have a wonderful wife, family and church. But I know it is a drop in the bucket compared to what God has in store for me. Therefore, I am determined to never forget, to always remember and to always worship with the heart of a true worshipper.

The most valuable thing I possess is the presence of God. Without that, nothing is worth anything. His presence is the core of my being.

We can't afford to ever forget where our wealth really comes from.

Healthy, Wealthy & Wise

God can restore anything in your life, even regenerate it. That means He can bring things in your life back to their original design. He can take relationships and situations back to the way He originally made them, to the place when they were good.

In every area of your life, He can do this for you. He wants to do this for you. He's eager to bless you and increase you. He's eager to give you more than enough with plenty left over. He wants you healthy, wealthy and wise.

These are the last days. You are part of the last days Church, the Church that will see the outpouring of God like no other generation.

Isaiah 45 records the words of King Cyrus, a gentile king who was in covenant with Israel. Cyrus represents the Church God wants to bless during the last days when the fullness of the Gentiles (the unsaved) will be brought into the Church as described in Romans 10.

In Isaiah 45:2-3, God said to Cyrus: "I will go before you and make the crooked places straight; I will break in pieces the gates of bronze and cut the bars of iron. I will give you the treasures of darkness and hidden riches of secret places, that you may know that I, the Lord, Who call you by your name, Am the God of Israel" (*New King James Version*).[63]

This is what God wants to do for you. He is saying to you: "I want to bless you with all this so that you'll know I'm the God of Israel, so that you'll know you were saved by grace, so that you'll know the favor of God is in your life, so that you know it's not by works."

Worship Him and honor Him from a pure heart.

Passionately love the presence of God.

Always remember where your wealth comes from.

Chapter 8

Always Hold Out For the Best

One time, when I was small, my parents were in a season of not having a lot of money. Their monthly budget was tight, but they needed a new car. So my dad did something he'd never done before. He bought a new car with zippo options. It had absolutely no frills. It was a bare necessities kind of car. In other words, the seat and steering wheel were the options.

My mom tells me that after he bought it, he was so discouraged when he made the payments that he decided he would never do that again. He figured if he had to make payments on something, it had better be something he really wanted.

As you accrue wealth in life, you will be tempted just as my dad was. You will be tempted to give up or give in way too soon.

That's not God's way.

God wants you to hold out for the best in life. He doesn't want you to give up before the blessing comes.

It's so easy to get off the path God has for your life...to take a little path here and a little path there, until you are in a big mess. It's easy to detour onto the path of least resistance, which always seems to be "good enough." But it will only be good enough for that moment, and as time marches on, you will be frustrated that you didn't hold out for God's best.

God really does want you to have more than enough with plenty left over—not just enough with a little bit left over.

He wants you to spiritually have more than enough with plenty left over. He wants you to have plenty of love, joy, happiness and contentment. He wants to remove the sorrows in your life and flood those places with the blessings of the future.

But you have to be willing to hold out for the best.

Choose the Best and Be the Best

Right before the children of Israel went into The Promised Land, God told them something critical to their success—and to yours.

He said, "I have set before you life and death, blessings and curses. Now choose life..." (Deuteronomy 30:19, *New International Version*).[64]

Choose means "to choose the best part; to choose the best part of the highest quality available."

There was a choice on the road up ahead for the children of Israel: blessing or cursing, life or death.

There's a constant choice every day for us as well.

If we don't choose the best for our lives, then we're actually choosing cursing and death every time.

Every person I've ever known that settled for "just enough"—with no exception—within a period of time, they would always be under some kind of curse. They would always be under something that was dominating or controlling them. There is a consequence to not reaching for and stretching for the best.

That's what that car payment was in my dad's life. It controlled him. He wasn't in control because he settled for just enough.

Don't get caught in the trap of settling for "just enough" because you believe God doesn't have anything better for you. God always has something great for your life.

When you're choosing a husband or a wife, don't settle for just any person who is available. Hold out for the best. When you're deciding on a career, don't just get a job. Get a life! Be ambitious. Have desire and set goals. Be the best at whatever you choose to become.

Do whatever you do with all your heart, as unto the Lord. Colossians 3:23 tells us, "And whatever you do, do it heartily, as to the Lord and not to men" (*New King James Version*).[65]

In other words, give it all you've got. Choose the best and be the best.

In other words, give it all you've got. Choose the best and be the best.

King David Gave His Best

Before King David died, he made abundant preparations for the temple to be rebuilt in Jerusalem—just as the Lord had commanded him. First Chronicles 22:5 records David's words: " 'My son Solomon is young and inexperienced, and the house to be built for the LORD should be of great magnificence and fame and splendor in the sight of all the nations. Therefore I will make preparations for it.' So David made extensive preparations before his death" (*New International Version*).[66]

David personally gave 100,000 talents of gold and 1 million talents of silver (1 Chronicles 22:14).[67] One talent weighs 75.6 pounds, so that's a lot of money! Dollar-wise, it would be worth $44.9 billion today. That's like blowing Fort Knox apart!

Why did David give so much?

Because he gave his best—and we are to do the same.

Haggai 2:7-9 prophesies that in the latter days, the glory of the temple will be greater than the former days: " 'I will fill this temple with glory,' says the LORD of hosts. 'The silver is Mine, and the gold is Mine,' says the LORD of hosts. 'The glory of this latter temple shall be greater than the former,' says the LORD of hosts" (*New King James Version*).[68]

The former days were David's day.

The latter days are ours.

We are the temple of the Lord!

What God has for the Church today will far surpass the awesomeness of what He did for the Israelites. The glory of the Church today will be much greater than what the Israelites experienced in the temple David commissioned. And that glory is not limited to the spiritual. It will be in our natural finances as well.

The Arrow Is In Your Hand

Remember the miracle of the prophet Elisha and the widow woman who filled the vessels of oil?[69] I mentioned it in Chapter 3. The woman was a widow with two sons whose husband had left her with an enormous debt. Her husband's creditors were coming for her sons to take them into slavery if she didn't come up with some money.

So she went to Elisha for help.

Elisha asked her what she had, which was one cruse of oil. He told her to borrow vessels from her neighbors and then begin pouring the oil into them. She filled all the vessels she had gathered and then the flow of oil stopped.

Then Elisha told her to sell all the oil, pay off the debts and live off the rest. She couldn't have been more than 25 or 30, so it must have been an extreme amount of money that she made off the oil.

Here is what I want you to notice: The prophet told her specifically what to do to stretch her faith. Later on in Elisha's life, when he was dying, King Johoash came to him concerned he would no longer get Words from God from Elisha and be able to defeat his enemies. Elisha had been his ace in the hole for years.

Elisha said to him, "Take that bow and arrow and shoot an arrow out the window. That represents your deliverance. Go ahead and shoot it in the ground. Every time you shoot, you've got deliverance" (2 Kings 13, my paraphrase).[70]

King Johoash shot three arrows out the window and into the ground and stopped.

Elisha said, "You should have shot it five or six times and completely destroyed your enemy."

Why did God, through the Prophet Elisha, tell the woman exactly what to do, but leave it up to the king whether he got a partial victory or a complete victory? What is the difference between these two miracles?

At first, the only difference I could see is that one was a widow and one was a king. That's the obvious.

But then I gained understanding.

Jesus said, "...to whom **much is given**, from him much will be required" (Luke 12:48, *New King James Version*).[71] "But many who are first will be last; and the last first" (Matthew 19:30 *New King James Version*).[72]

When we were born again, God took us from the back of the line and moved us to the front of the line. In Ephesians 2:6 says He has "raised us up together, and made us sit together in heavenly places in Christ Jesus."[73] Revelation 1:6 says He has "made us kings and priests."[74]

We are responsible to reign over the areas of dominion God has entrusted to us.

We have already been given much, and much is required of us. We will have to choose the complete victory. We have been given king status, and with that status comes responsibility. We are responsible to reign over the areas of dominion God has entrusted to us.

The arrow is in your hand. You have been baptized in the name of Jesus Christ. You have the authority of Jesus Christ. You have been instructed to "resist the devil" and promised that "he will flee" (James 4:7).[75] There is no scripture that says Jesus will resist the devil for you.

"You stand steadfast in the faith. You resist the devil" (1 Corinthians 15:58;[76] Colossians 1:23;[77] Ephesians 6:11-14;[78] 1 Corinthians 16:13;[79] James 4:7).[75] That's what God's Word says.

Having the best in life is up to you—no one else.

Having more than enough with plenty left over is up to you—no one else.

Focus on Your Victories

I read an article once about a famous painter who lacked self-confidence—despite his success. So, to encourage himself, he kept a remarkable painting of roses he had created for himself. He had many serious offers for this particular painting, but he kept it for himself, and when he would be discouraged, he would examine this work of art and say, "I painted that." As he did, his confidence would rise to the surface. He knew deep down that if he had done it once, he could do it again and again and again.

> *Having the best in life is up to you—no one else.*
> *Having more than enough with plenty left over is up to you—no one else.*

Some of you reading this book have prayed for your children and seen them turn around. You've seen them healed and set free. You've prayed for money and the bills got paid. You've prayed for all kinds of needs, and the answers came.

Focus on those times. Focus on the victories.

We all have defeats, but don't think on those. We all have bad experiences that try to define us. They are called memories. But don't focus on those.

Focus on the victories and develop your faith for the areas you need to overcome. Faith believes to the point it knows, "I'm going to do it! I'm just going to do it."

Noah built an ark because of one word from God—and then he waited 120 years for the second word. But he started and finished building the ark based on the first word.

First Peter 1:9 says, "Receiving the end of your faith, the salvation of your souls." (*New King James Version*)[80] *Receive* in this verse means "to obtain the end of your faith."

When you believe, obtain the end of your faith. Bring it all the way from the spiritual realm into the physical realm. Bring your healing, your prosperity, your restored relationships. Bring it all. Hold out for the best.

Hold Out For Reinforcements

Remember all those old western movie scenes where the good guys are in a fort, and the bad guys are shooting like crazy at them? The good guys in the fort are running out of ammunition and supplies and they need some fast. The only problem is, to get more supplies and reinforcements, someone has to volunteer to run through the enemy lines and bring back help.

So, usually at night, a good guy sneaks out, crawling out on his belly only to break out into a fierce run.

Then the good guys spend agonizing days wondering, *Did he make it? Will anyone come to help?*

Sometimes believing can feel that way. *Did my faith make it through? Will the manifestation come? Can we hold out until it does?*

Yes you can if you'll follow these principles in God's Word:

First, stay in fellowship with God. When you are believing for more than enough with plenty left over, don't let your flesh dominate and control you. Yield to the Spirit of God and His character living on the inside of you. Don't let jealousy, envy, strife, greed, lust or anything else control you. That means don't feed them.

A great illustration of this is my dog, Chewy. He's the most professional beggar I know. If you come to my house and are offered dessert, Chewy will sit there looking at you breathing really heavily. He'll sit up on his tail with his front paws bent downward like a real pro.

So what does Chewy have to do with your flesh? Everything. If you feed the flesh by the table of blessing, that flesh will always create a habit of continually flaring up in your life.

By feeding it, I mean feeding jealousy by talking about it, feeding unforgiveness by talking about it, feeding greed and lust by talking about it. If you feed bad habits they will always be there begging at your table, and those habits will keep you out of fellowship with God. Those habits will keep you from what

God wants you to walk in. Those habits will keep you from having the best. They will keep you from having more than enough with plenty left over.

Thank God His grace is greater than broken fellowship.

All you have to say to make changes and hold out for the best is to say, "No, dog. I'm not feeding you!"

Second, cast down every thought and vain imagination (2 Corinthians 10:5).[81] Whenever I am in a trial, and I find that I'm losing my peace of mind, I immediately seek God for understanding, because when I gain understanding, I know which thoughts have exalted themselves against Christ and which thoughts are good. Without God's understanding, it's easy to think that the way I'm thinking is OK, when it's not. You've got to think right to believe right.

When you pray and ask God for understanding, He will always give it to you. James 1:5 promises us, "If any of you lacks wisdom, he should ask God, who gives generously to all without finding fault, and it will be given to him" (*New International Version*).[82]

When you need wisdom and understanding, ask for it. Search the scriptures and spend time in prayer. Then anticipate God speaking to you. He'll give you peace with His wisdom, because there is always peace with wisdom, always peace with understanding.

He wants you to want what His Word has outlined for your life.

God Wants to Give You What You Want

God really does want to give you what you want—not what He wants. But He wants you to want what His Word has outlined for your life. He wants you to want what is in agreement with His will—because it is what is perfect for your life.

I mentioned this in Chapter 4, but it bears repeating if you are holding out for God's best. First John 5:14 says, "This is the confidence we have in approaching God: that if we ask anything *according to his will,* he hears us. And if we know that he hears us–whatever we ask–we know that we have what we asked of him" (1 John 5:14-15, *New International Version*).[83]

Jesus said, "If you abide in Me, and My words abide in you"—[if your actions line up with My Word]—"you will ask what you desire, and it shall be done for you" (John 15:7, *New King James Version*).[84]

God is saying through Jesus, "I want you to line up with My Word so that you can have what you want, because what you want—if you line up with My Word—is what I want for you."

God doesn't care what car or house you want. He's more than willing to give it to you. He just wants you to abide in Him. He wants you to have fellowship with Him. He loves you and wants to bless you, but before He blesses you, He wants your heart.

God wants the best for your life. He wants to honor your faithfulness and reward you with all good things. He wants to move you from the end of the line to the front of the line. He wants you to have an eye for excellence, and a taste for all that is good. He wants you to worship Him as He heaps blessings after blessings on your life. He wants you to always hold out for His best. He wants you to ALWAYS have more than enough with plenty left over.

About the Author

Jack Holt is the senior pastor and founder of River of Life Fellowship, a vibrant non-denominational church of more than 2000 people in Kent, Washington. He is a graduate of Rhema Bible College, Tulsa, Oklahoma, and holds a Ministerial Studies diploma from Berean University, Springfield, Missouri. He also has completed studies in Hebrew and Greek.

Jack's preaching and teaching is characterized by life-changing truths and powerfully motivating messages that build faith and energize Christians to live fulfilled and victorious lives. His encouraging television program, *Running the Race to Win,* is seen by thousands of viewers every week.

He and his wife, Joyce, have two grown children and live in Kent, Washington.

For more information contact the ministry of Pastor Jack Holt on the internet at:
www.riveroflifefellowship.org
or by writing to:
River of Life Fellowship
10615 SE 216th Street
Kent, Washington 98031
Or by calling: 253-859-0832

Scripture References

CHAPTER 1
God Really Wants You to Have
*More Than Enough With
Plenty Leftover*

(1) Psalm 34:10 (*New King James Version*)
(2) Psalm 84:11 (*New King James Version*)
(3) Psalm 23:1 (*New King James Version*)
(4) John 15:7 (*New King James Version*)

CHAPTER 2
God's Dream For Your Life

(5) Jeremiah 29:11 (*New International Version*)
(6) Matthew 6:33 (*New King James Version*)
(7) Psalm 37:4 (*New International Version*)
(8) Malachi 3:11 (*New King James Version*)
(9) Psalm 91:9-12 (*New International Version*)
(10) 1 Timothy 6:9-10 (*New International Version*)
(11) Proverbs 10:22 (*New King James Version*)
(12) 2 Corinthians 9:8 (*New King James Version*)
(13) 1 Timothy 6:6-7 (*New International Version*)
(14) 2 Peter 1:3 (*New American Standard*)

(15) 1 Timothy 6:8 (*New International Version*)
(16) 2 Corinthians 9:7 (*New International Version*)
(17) 1 Timothy 6:17-19 (*New King James Version*)

CHAPTER 3
Accruing More Than Enough–
It's a Process

(18) Colossians 3:23 (*New King James Version*)
(19) John 15:7 (*New King James Version*)
(20) Philippians 2:13 (*New American Standard*)
(21) 1 John 3:22 (*New American Standard*)
(22) Romans 10:17 (*New American Standard*)
(23) Isaiah 1:19 (*New King James Version*)
(24) Psalm 127:1 (*New International Version*)
(25) James 4:3 (*King James Version*)
(26) Luke 2:52 (*New International Version*)
(27) 2 Kings 4:1-7 (*New International Version*)

CHAPTER 4
Faithfulness–
It Expedites the Process

(28) Genesis 12:2 (*New King James Version*)
(29) Matthew 25:14-18 (*New King James Version*)
(30) Matthew 25:19-29 (*New King James Version*)
(31) Proverbs 28:20 (*New King James Version*)
(32) Deut. 28:2 (*New American Standard Version*)
(33) Proverbs 20:6 (*New King James Version*)
(34) 1 Corinthians 4:2 (*New King James Version*)

CHAPTER 5
How God Rewards You

(35) Hebrews 11:6 (*New King James Version*)
(36) Psalm 34:10 (*New King James Version*)
(37) Psalm 37:4 (*New King James Version*)
(38) John 15:7 (*New King James Version*)
(39) Ephesians 6:5-8 (*King James Version*)
(40) Luke 13:6-9 (*New King James Version*)
(41) John 15:5-8 (*New International Version*)
(42) 1 Corinthians 3:10-15 (*New International Version*)
(43) Acts 20:35 (*New International Version*)
(44) 1 John 5:14-15 (*New International Version*)

CHAPTER 6
God Wants You to Have
Quality *and* Quantity

(45) Numbers 13:23-24 (*New International Version*)
(46) John 2:4-10 (*New International Version*)
(47) Psalm 34:8 and 10 (*New King James Version*)
(48) Proverbs 28:20 (*New King James Version*)
(49) 2 Peter 1:5 (*New King James Version*)
(50) James 5:17 (*New International Version*)
(51) James 5:16 (*New King James Version*)
(52) James 2:26 (*New King James Version*)
(53) Mark 4:13-20 (*New International Version*)
(54) 2 Corinthians 9:6 (*New King James Version*)
(55) Matthew 20:1-16 (*New King James Version*)
(56) 2 Peter 1:3 (*New King James Version*)
(57) Ephesians 1:3 (*New King James Version*)
(58) Psalm 23:4-6 (*New King James Version*)

CHAPTER 7
Remember Where Your
Wealth Comes From

(59) John 2:11 (*New King James Version*)
(60) Psalm 42 (*New King James Version*)
(61) 1 Corinthians 3:16-17 (*New King James Version*)
(62) Psalm 84:10 (*New International Version*)
(63) Isaiah 45:2-3 (*New King James Version*)

CHAPTER 8
Always Hold Out For the Best

(64) Deuteronomy 30:19 (*New International Version*)
(65) Colossians 3:23 (*New King James Version*)
(66) 1 Chronicles 22:5 (*New International Version*)
(67) 1 Chronicles 22:14 (*New King James Version*)
(68) Haggai 2:7-9 (*New King James Version*)
(69) 2 Kings 4:1-7 (*New International Version*)
(70) 2 Kings 13:15-19 (*New King James Version*)
(71) Luke 12:48 (*New King James Version*)
(72) Matthew 19:30 (*New King James Version*)
(73) Ephesians 2:6 (*New King James Version*)
(74) Revelation 1:6 (*New King James Version*)
(75) James 4:7 (*New King James Version*)
(76) 1 Corinthians 15:58 (*New King James Version*)
(77) Colossians 1:23 (*New King James Version*)
(78) Ephesians 6:11-14 (*New King James Version*)
(79) 1 Corinthians 16:13 (*New King James Version*)
(80) 1 Peter 1:9 (*New King James Version*)
(81) 2 Corinthians 10:5 (*New King James Version*)
(82) James 1:5 (*New International Version*)
(83) 1 John 5:14-15 (*New International Version*)
(84) John 15:7 (*New King James Version*)

More Resources from Jack Holt Ministries:

STAYING POSITIVE IN A NEGATIVE WORLD

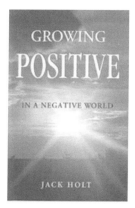 It's easy to get caught up in the whirl-wind of negativity as our world is constantly changing. Even in the midst of bad circumstances, we can remain in a place of blessing and free-dom. Pastor Jack Holt shares some how-to's that will liberate you from negativity and bring you into a ful-filling life as a champion of God. It is completely possible to conquer the challenges you face and walk in vic-tory by applying the truths set forth in this refreshing and straight-forward book.

Order# B1001

PUTTING AN END TO DEAD ENDS

Stop sabotaging yourself of the victory that God has planned for you! Learn what may be keeping you from achieving all that you can in Christ. This 4-CD audio series explains how to eliminate "dead end think-ing" and how to step into the place of expectancy.

Order# A1007

More Resources from Jack Holt Ministries:

YOUR TONGUE-MASTER KEY TO ALL BLESSINGS

The Bible is clear that by our words we will be justified or condemned. Don't let your words rob you of a fruitful existence. This 6-CD audio series will give you great insight to the importance of controlling that powerful member of our bodies - the tongue - as described in James 3:5.

Order# A1234

STAYING STEADY

Oftentimes we quit the fight just before God pours out the blessings He has for us. Learn the importance behind commitment and how to remain on track with the Word and the will of God in this 4-CD audio series.

Order# A1006

More Resources from Jack Holt Ministries:

Individual Audio Messages

These individual teachings are invaluable to your walk with Christ. CD's may be purchased for $5.50 each. Cassettes can be purchased for $4.50 each. Prices include shipping and handling. When ordering, please specify CD or cassette.

FAITH

The Law of Expectancy	2918
Staking Your Claim to the Promises	3022
Changing Your Life Through the Spoken Word	3028
You Can Break the Cycle of Defeat	3029
Settling for the Right Things	3039
Controlling Your Circumstances	3226
Closing the Door to Trouble	3231

RIGHT THINKING

Rooting Out Fear	2931
Mental Barriers	3044
Breaking the Cycle of Negative Thinking	3045
Thinking that Doesn't Hold You Back	3047
Refusing to Quit	3056
Driving Out the Doubt	3079
Changing Your End Results	3229

More Resources from Jack Holt Ministries:

Individual Audio Messages

EXPECTATION

Is it Still Possible to Do the Impossible?	3059
Lifting Up Your Expectations	3067
High Expectancy	3073
Taking Off the Limits	3075
Passionate Expectations	3076
Living Off the Overflow	3222
Hope, the Place of Exchange	3224
Receiving Power	3227

CHARACTER

Commitment Takes You to the Top	2869
Anointed to Serve	2876
Adjusting Your Attitude	2896
Refusing to Quit	2964
Unlocking the Blessing	3208

VISION

Breaking Free from Things that Hold You Back	2983
If God's in it, Don't Quit	2984
The Expected End	2986
Never Say Never	2994
The Law of Breakthrough	2995

To order or view more products, please visit **www.jackholtministries.org**. To receive JHM's free newsletter, *Running the Race to Win*, please contact us at: **Jack Holt Ministries**, 10615 SE 216th Street, Kent, WA 98031 or call 253-859-0832

To order additional copies of

More Than Enough

With Plenty Left Over

Contact our Website Bookstore:
              www.riveroflifefellowship.org

OR call: 253-859-0832

Mail order: Jack Holt Ministries
                River of Life Fellowship
                10615 SE 216th Street
                Kent, WA. 98031

Please include your name, address, and phone number
with your check or money order.

Book Price: $11.99

Shipping: $3.00 for the first book and $1.00 for each
additional book to cover shipping and handling
within US, Canada, and Mexico. International or-
ders add $6.00 for the first book and $2.00 for each
additional book.